SOUNDS YOU CANNOT HEAR

SOUNDS
YOU
CANNOT
HEAR

BY ERIC WINDLE

ILLUSTRATED BY JOHN KAUFMANN

PRENTICE-HALL, INC., ENGLEWOOD CLIFFS, N. J.

Prentice-Hall International, Inc.
London · Tokyo · Sydney · Paris

Prentice-Hall of Canada, Ltd.
Prentice-Hall de Mexico, S.A.

to EMMY

CONTENTS

SOUNDS
YOU
CANNOT
HEAR

1.

SILENT SOUND

Have you ever seen a dog come scampering home when his master called him with a "dog whistle"? You may have seen the dog racing home, but you could not have heard the sound that was calling him.

There are some sounds you cannot hear at all—whether you want to or not. But there are many kinds of animals that *can* hear these "silent sounds," and they make use of them in many ways.

Guiding themselves by sounds we cannot hear, bats can swoop around their dark cave-homes without bumping into one another or without crashing into the walls. Bats "fly blind" by using sound waves that *you* cannot hear.

Many creatures of the sea find their way in the total darkness of the deepest parts of the ocean by using

11

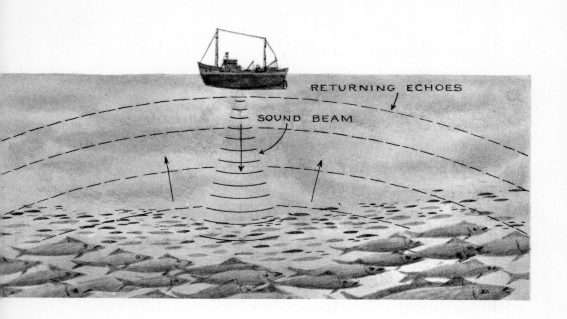

RETURNING ECHOES

SOUND BEAM

silent sound. Scientists think that many of them are guided by sound waves above the range of human hearing.

Today, man has learned to make use of silent sound. He has put it to work in many wonderful ways.

Fishermen send beams of silent sound speeding into the ocean's depths. Returning *echoes*—sound waves that bounce back to the sender—help the fishermen locate schools of fish. Silent sound even "tells" the fishermen if the fish in the school are large or small— large fish cause stronger return signals, or echoes, than small fish.

Scientists have discovered that sound waves, unheard by us, can kill tiny but harmful bacteria in water, milk, medicine, and foods. There is still much to be learned about how and why this happens.

Silent sound is also proving very helpful in ridding man of one of his most deadly and ancient pests—the rat. Rat-infested places can be cleared with blasts of silent sound. Rats' ears are very sensitive to such sound. It actually *hurts* their ears. Unwanted rats run away when beams of speeding sound are aimed at their hiding places.

A burglar alarm has been invented that can send silent sound waves through a bank. If a burglar enters the bank and "disturbs" the waves an alarm is automatically set off.

The study and use of sound waves that are above the range of human hearing is called *ultrasonics*. It is one of the newest sciences to be explored by man. *Ultra* is a Latin word. It means *beyond the normal range or limit*. *Sonic* comes from the Latin word *sonus*, meaning *sound*. So ultrasonic means sound beyond that which we can normally hear.

New uses for ultrasonics are being discovered each day. But "clues" to its possible uses have been known for a long time. For several hundred years, a scientist here, and a scientist there, had found some fact about ultrasonics. These facts lay about like the jumbled pieces of a jigsaw puzzle. It was not until World War I that scientists were able to put the pieces together.

2.
HOW
IT ALL BEGAN

One of the first scientists to give us an important clue to the science of ultrasonics was Lazzaro Spallanzani (Spahl-lahn-ZAH-nee), an Italian biologist, who worked with animals. In 1793 he became interested in the flight of bats, and he spent many hours watching a colony of bats that lived in a bell tower.

Spallanzani soon realized that the bats slept all day and flew only at night. He began to wonder how they were able to fly about in the total darkness of the bell tower without crashing into one another.

He came to believe that bats were able to fly blind. Spallanzani was sure that the bats could not see in the dark. But if they could not see when it was dark, how could they fly without crash-landing?

To prove that bats could fly blind, Spallanzani captured and blinded several bats, and allowed them to fly away. He waited four days and then rounded up some of his blinded bats.

When he examined their stomachs he found that the blinded bats had caught as many insects as "sighted" bats. He had proved that bats did not depend on their sight to guide their flight or to hunt. Spallanzani strongly suspected that bats "saw" with their ears. But how could he prove it?

To prove his theory that bats saw with their ears, Spallanzani captured other sighted bats. He plugged the ears of these sighted bats and released them in his living room.

They took off—and crash, slam, crunch—the "deaf" bats bumped into walls, tables, and chairs. They slammed into one another, and crash-landed on the floor.

16

Spallanzani had proved his theory that bats used their ears to guide their flight. It was over one hundred years before other scientists found out *how* bats "saw" with their *ears!*

The first major use of ultrasonics by man grew out of the need to defend our country during World War I. In 1917, a French scientist named Paul Langevin (Lanj-VAN) invented equipment that used ultrasonics to locate enemy submarines.

The engineers who thought of using ultrasonics in defense paid little attention to the animal research that Spallanzani and others had done, and it was not until 1938 that the early ideas of Spallanzani were proved to be true. Let's see how this came to pass.

There was a student at Harvard University, named Donald R. Griffin, who was very interested in bats. He knew that a Harvard professor, Dr. G. W. Pierce, had developed an electronic machine which could pick up sound waves that were beyond human hearing.

One day the young student started across the Harvard campus with a cage of bats. He was headed for the laboratory of Professor Pierce. There, for the first time, the ultrasonic clicks and squeaks which bats use for navigation were heard over the professor's machine.

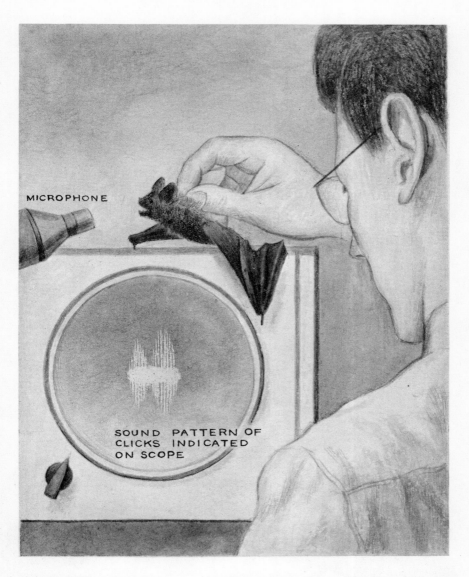

MICROPHONE

SOUND PATTERN OF
CLICKS INDICATED
ON SCOPE

DONALD R. GRIFFIN - HARVARD UNIVERSITY - 1938

Since then, scientists have learned much more about how animals make use of ultrasonics.

Did you know that crickets "talk" to each other with ultrasonics? Such sounds are made by the scraping action of the crickets' wings.

Did you know that rats play games? While playing, they open their mouths very wide and scream at the top of their voices. But their screams are beyond our hearing limits.

Ultrasonics is now a rapidly-growing science. But before you can really understand ultrasonics—sounds you cannot hear—it is important to know more about sounds you *can* hear.

3.

SOUNDS UNLIMITED

Have you ever tried to find out how many different sounds you can hear in five minutes? If you haven't, try it.

Sit absolutely quiet and listen. How many different sounds did you hear? Actually, all of us hear hundreds of sounds every day.

Sound has been a part of our world since time began. Some of the sounds you hear today were heard by your great-great-grandparents.

How do we know that there is such a thing as sound? You're right! We know that sound exists because we can hear it. But just because we can *hear* sound does not mean that we know what sound really *is*. Let's see if we can find out what sound really *is*.

Imagine that we are visiting a world where there is *no* sound. In this make-believe world everything is silent. But why? There is no sound because there is no *motion*. Nothing is moving—anywhere. The leaves hang motionless from the branches. We do not hear them rustle in the wind because there is no wind. There is not even the gentle sound of a whispered secret.

Our earth is full of sound because it is full of motion— jets zoom into the sky, trucks roll along the highway, and people do all sorts of noisy things.

Sometimes a sound is very close, like the buzzing of a hornet flying around your head.

Other sounds are far away and yet you are often able to hear them clearly. You may hear the whirling of a helicopter hovering so far above the earth that you can barely see it.

Do you know how such faraway sounds travel toward our ears? This, too, has something to do with motion.

All sound travels to our ears in about the same way. It comes to us in *waves*, not unlike the waves in water.

Have you ever noticed how smooth and still a lake is on a calm day? Smooth, still water acts like a mirror. You are able to look into the water and see a reflection, or picture, of yourself. Drop a pebble into the water. What happens?

WAVE MOTIONS

SOUND IN AIR

RINGS IN WATER

As the pebble splashes into the water, something will begin to move. You will see rings or waves moving away from where the pebble hit the water.

Try to imagine that real sound waves look like the rings or waves on the water. But remember, you actually cannot *see* sound waves without special electronic equipment. The behavior of sound waves can be seen on a screen somewhat like the picture tube of a television set.

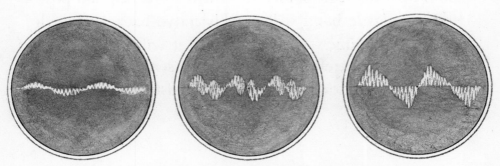

SOUND WAVES ON ELECTRONIC SCREENS

Most of the sound waves that reach your ears travel through the air, but sound can also travel through water. The sound waves of an explosion several miles away move through the air to your ears. And if you knock two stones together under water, the sound will travel through the water to your ears.

Sound also moves through solids. Try scratching one end of a long stick as you hold the other end to one of your ears. The sound will actually move through the stick. Perhaps you have heard sound travel through the walls of a house from one room to another.

We know that sound moves and travels. But what kind of movement causes sound waves to start traveling outward in all directions?

Sound is caused by *vibrations*. A vibration is simply a back and forth movement.

Try this: Stretch an elastic band tightly between two nails that are fastened to a wooden board. Pull back on the band. When you let go, it will suddenly jump forward. But before it returns to its original position the elastic band will quickly move back and forth a number of times—in other words, it will vibrate.

Look very carefully and you will see that this happens within a few seconds. If you listen closely, you

may hear the faint humming sound made by the vibrations.

When you speak, your vocal cords act much like a vibrating elastic band. They move back and forth. The strings of a violin or a banjo also vibrate to make sound.

If you place your hands gently on a bass drum when it is being played, you will feel the sound vibrations.

Next time a large, heavy truck passes by, stand still on the sidewalk for a moment. You will feel the vibrations under your feet.

It is such vibrations that make sound waves. Strong vibrations make *loud* sounds. Weak vibrations make *soft* sounds.

4.

QUIET NOISE

Do you visit at your best friend's house often? If you do, you are a *frequent* visitor—you go there often. The word frequent tells us that something is repeated again and again.

The number of times a second that a vibration is repeated is called its *frequency.* When a man's vocal cords vibrate slowly, we say it causes *low-frequency* sound. This gives the man a deep voice.

Such slow vibrations make a small number of sound waves each second. Another name for low-frequency sounds is *low-pitched* sounds. They have low tones like the deep roar of thunder.

High-frequency sound, like a canary's song, is caused by rapid vibrations which make a great number of sound waves each second. This is also called *high-pitched* sound.

The shrill siren of a fire engine is a sound with a high pitch. What high-frequency sounds have you heard lately?

Peoples' ears are usually able to hear sounds that have frequencies as low as fifteen vibrations a second. Most people can hear sounds that have frequencies as high as twenty thousand vibrations a second.

But human ears are not able to pick up very low-pitched sounds or extremely high-pitched sounds. Our ears pick up sounds much as a radio receiver picks up radio waves. Most radio receivers can pick up radio waves from stations which send out messages on certain frequencies.

You should know another important fact about sound. It has to do with *intensity*. The intensity of a sound means its strength or loudness.

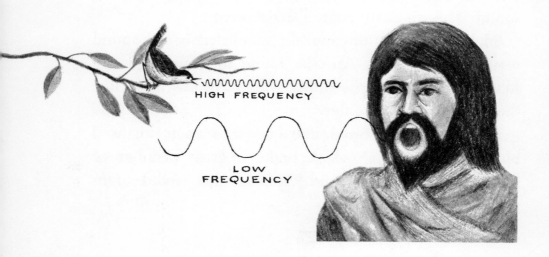

HIGH FREQUENCY

LOW FREQUENCY

H
I
G
H

INTENSITY OF SOUND

L
O
W

Strong vibrations make strong sounds. Beating a drum or blowing a trumpet makes strong vibrations which result in strong, *intense* sound.

Weak vibrations cause weak sounds of low intensity. Writing with a pencil makes weak vibrations. You would have to listen carefully to hear the weak, scratching sound that a pencil makes as you write.

The motion of blinking your eyes makes an even weaker, less intense sound. If you blink rapidly and listen hard, you might hear a slight clicking sound.

Can you think of any low-intensity sounds? The quiet stalking of a leopard as he creeps up to his prey is a low-intensity sound. Actually, cats do make some noise, but the sound is usually much too weak for our ears to pick up. It is sound of a very low intensity.

29

Do you think that ants make much noise? If you study an ant colony carefully, you will discover that the ants are busy scurrying about building ant hills or carrying food to their colony. But we don't hear them working. We hear nothing, even when the thousands of ants in an ant hill eat breakfast each morning. They too make sound of very low intensity.

Scientists have made studies of the sounds that small animals make. They have heard crunching, clicking, grinding, and squeaking sounds. But scientists are only able to hear these sounds when they use special equipment to *amplify*, or to make the sounds louder.

There are probably millions of tiny sounds all around you that you cannot hear. Your ears are not made to pick up sounds of very low intensity.

The distance from which you hear a sound has a great deal to do with its intensity.

Let's think back for a moment to the example of dropping a pebble into the water. Do you remember what happened? Ring-shaped waves moved away from the pebble. As the waves traveled farther away from the pebble, they grew wider. But as the waves grew larger and covered more space, they became weaker. The outside waves were not as easy to see as the waves close to the center, where the pebble landed.

The same thing happens with sound waves. The farther out they spread, the weaker and less loud they become.

When you are very close to the place where a sound actually started, you can hear it better. This is because the sound waves are stronger. But when you are several miles away from an explosion, it does not seem very loud to your ears. This is because the sound waves became much weaker as they traveled away from the exact place where the explosion was set off.

At an airport, the roar of airplanes before take-off is so loud that it almost hurts your ears. The sound is much louder than that of a plane flying overhead in the sky. By the time the sound from the plane in the sky has traveled to the ground, it has become much weaker.

There are all kinds of sounds about us all the time— high and low, loud and soft, near and far.

5.

NIGHT HUNTER

Now that we have a good idea of how the sounds we *can* hear come to us, we are ready to find out how bats make use of ultrasonics—the sounds we cannot hear.

The little brown bat soars across the sky in search of food. In a flash of speed, he heads straight toward his unseen target. Within a few seconds he is eating a tasty insect, and then another, and another.

Each night, in the warm weather, the little brown bat hunts for insects. He is able to catch an insect every six seconds; and he seldom misses. His favorite diet is a three-course dinner of moths, mosquitoes, and beetles.

This tiny animal spends all day hanging upside down in the hollow tree which is his home. Some of his bat friends live in nearby caves and bell towers.

BAT SONAR

We know that bats have very poor sight. They would not be able to catch insects if they depended on their eyes for flying and hunting at night.

But bats have special equipment to tell them where to fly and where to find food. They guide themselves with their voices and with their ears. Bats have excellent hearing. Some bats have huge ears that are shaped like funnels. Sounds hit these big ears and "pour" into the bat's inner ear.

You remember that Spallanzani proved that bats use their keen hearing to help them fly blind. But *how* do bats *see* with their *ears?*

You already know that bats make sounds you cannot hear. As they fly through the air, they make many tiny clicking and squeaking sounds. The squeaking sounds are of a very high frequency. They are sometimes caused by vibrations as fast as 130,000 times per second.

Bats send out ultrasonic cries through the air, one after another. When they do this, something very strange happens. It has something to do with *echoes*. Echoes are sounds that bounce back to us like a rubber ball that has been thrown against a wall.

Have you ever heard an echo of your voice? Try to imagine that you are standing some distance away from a high cliff. You face toward the cliff and shout:

HELLO! as loud as you can. Then count—one second, two seconds. At the end of two seconds you hear the faint echo of your HELLO! which has bounced back to you from the walls of the cliff.

When you shout hello, the sound waves of your voice go speeding toward the cliff. The waves hit the walls of the cliff and bounce back to where you are standing.

Sound waves usually travel through the air at the rate of about one thousand feet a second. If it took only two seconds for the sound to travel to the cliff and back again, you should be able to figure out about how far away from the cliff you were standing when you shouted.

Let's see if your figuring is right: The sound traveled to the cliff in one second. The other second was used

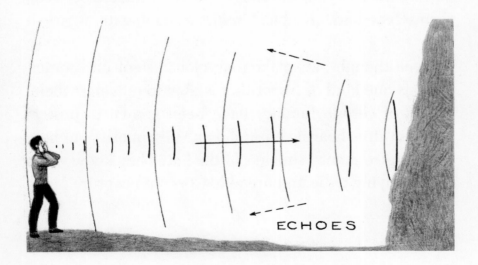

ECHOES

for the return trip. So if sound can travel about one thousand feet a second, the cliff was close to a thousand feet away.

If the cliff had been three thousand feet away from you, the journey of the sound waves would have taken three seconds each way. This would have been six seconds for the entire trip there and back.

Bats use echoes much as you use your voice when you are trying to get the bounce-back of an echo. Bats know how far away a wall or an insect is by sending out ultrasonic signals. Scientists believe that they can "judge" distance by the time it takes the echo of their voices to return.

You had to *figure out* what the distance between you and the cliff was by the time it took your echo to bounce back to you. But bats *know* the distance between themselves and an object *without* having to figure it out.

Even though bats make marvelous use of ultrasonics, there is one kind of insect that is able to outsmart them. Moths of certain families have been known to possess very sensitive hearing equipment. These moths can hear the high-frequency squeaks of the bat. They know when a bat is flying close and are able to escape capture.

6.

RADAR—
ELECTRONIC DETECTIVE

At this very moment, radio waves might be speeding through your body. Can you *hear* them? Can you *feel* them? You're right! The answer to both questions is *no*. We are not aware of the harmless radio waves that speed through our bodies and rush through the air all around us. Yet scientists have invented a way of using radio waves to detect, or help find, certain objects. Scientists make use of radio waves with an electronic detective called *radar,* which means *RAdio Detection And Ranging.*

Radar uses radio waves in about the same way that the bat uses sound waves. Radio waves can also echo back and tell where something is located.

Sound waves need something to travel through, such as solids, liquids, or air. Radio waves travel through the air. But, unlike sound waves, they can move through *outer space*.

Radio waves are made from electricity. Electrical energy is sent out as waves. The waves travel at the speed of light—about 186,000 miles a second.

Radar will be used to defend our country in case of an enemy attack. Radar stations are on the watch twenty-four hours a day. They will warn us of the approach of enemy aircraft. Flying radar stations, in long-range aircraft, are patrolling far off our shores.

A radar operator sends out radio waves, one after another. He then looks at a screen which is not unlike a television screen. This screen is called a *radarscope*. When the radio waves hit an airplane and bounce back as echoes, something suddenly happens on the scope. The echoes appear on the screen as bright spots or blobs of light. The best of the radarscopes go still further. They actually show the *shape* of an airplane.

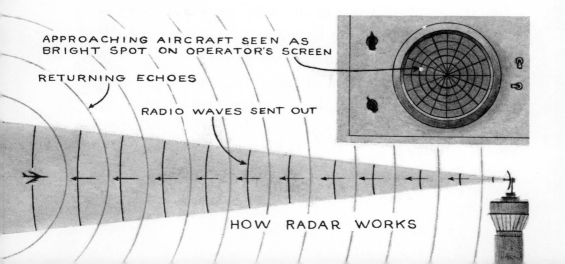

APPROACHING AIRCRAFT SEEN AS
BRIGHT SPOT ON OPERATOR'S SCREEN

RETURNING ECHOES

RADIO WAVES SENT OUT

HOW RADAR WORKS

Then an electronic computer "figures out" how far away the airplane is. The computing is automatic. The radar operator does nothing but wait for the answer.

Let's imagine that an airplane is approaching. Radio waves detect it some distance away. If it takes the radio waves one-thousandth of a second to travel to the airplane and echo back, then the distance to the airplane and back is one-thousandth of the speed of radio waves (about 186,000 miles a second). This is 186 miles.

But the radar operator needs to know the distance *one way*. So the computer gives the answer to one half of 186 miles. It reports that the airplane is 93 miles away.

One of the widest uses of radar is in air transportation. Jet airliners travel about 600 miles an hour. Smaller jets have set speed records of over 1,000 miles per hour.

Traveling at such high speeds makes the job of the pilot more difficult. He must know when objects, such as other aircraft, are in the way long before he gets close to them.

At high speed, a pilot might crash into a mountain only a few seconds after sighting it. A jet pilot *must* know about mountains ahead—in plenty of time. He must also be warned of dangerous air currents and storm clouds.

Landing in bad weather is a tricky task for any pilot. Even the smallest error can lead to disaster. Radar has

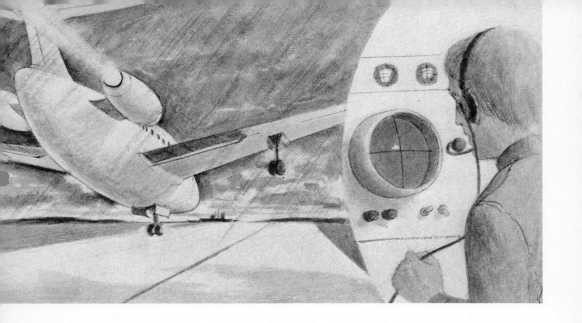

helped thousands of airmen to bring down their planes for a safe landing.

A radar operator on the ground guides the pilot straight down the middle of the landing strip. He talks to the pilot by radio to give him directions. Transportation on land has also become much safer, thanks to radar. It is used to detect speeding cars. Highway patrols can now detect a speeding car and stop a reckless driver *before* an accident occurs.

Radar plays an important part at the Weather Bureau, too. Radar echoes are used to locate and follow clouds and storms. When bad weather is located, people are warned to leave an area. Radar helps save lives by detecting hurricanes or tornadoes in time.

The space sciences also use radar. Using powerful radio transmitters with huge antennas, scientists send out radio waves toward objects in space. Careful study of the echoes that come back to earth gives astronomers new information about planets and other bodies in outer space.

The Army has already contacted the moon by radar. It took only two and one half seconds for the radio waves to travel to the moon and return. This is a round trip of 500,000 miles. And we have already bounced signals off man-made satellites as far off as 6,000 miles in space.

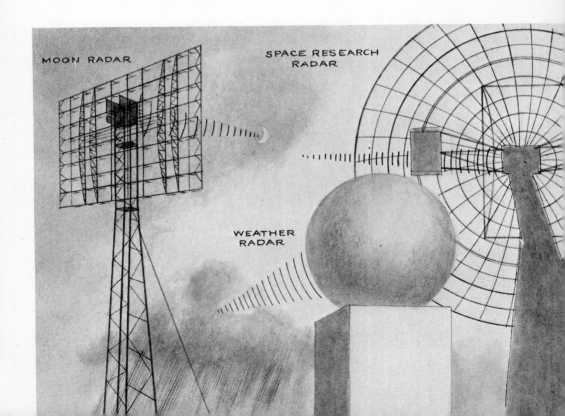

MOON RADAR

SPACE RESEARCH RADAR

WEATHER RADAR

Satellites are made in different sizes and shapes. Many of them look like huge balls with rows of tiny windows around the middle. They carry electronic equipment that receives and sends messages. This equipment is run by energy from the sun.

Have you ever listened to a short-wave radio that receives programs from other continents? You've probably had a hard time hearing because of the noisy "static." Sometimes long-distance programs fade away so that you cannot hear them at all. This is often caused by sun storms which affect the atmosphere. When the atmosphere is disturbed, so are the radio waves.

With the help of satellites, radio, telephone, and television signals can be sent from continent to continent. The first clear trans-Atlantic show to come to our home sets was bounced off the American satellite *Telstar* in July, 1962. Programs were broadcast from London, Paris, and New York City and were heard around the world.

Each day, man is learning more and more about ways to use echoes from space. But do you think there are echoes in the sea? Let's find out.

7.

ECHOES OF THE DEEP

Whalers often told whoppers about "talking creatures" of the deep seas.

Were these tales nothing but legends made up by seamen to help pass the time during long journeys? Or were these tall tales true? Do *talking* sea creatures really exist? Yes, they do.

Special equipment has been invented that records underwater sounds. Phonograph records of such sounds have been made and the "silent sea" is not silent.

There are many sounds below the surface of the water. And many of them are made by talking creatures. Some of these sounds are even louder than the roar of the surf beating against the rocks at the edge of a coastline. Perhaps there are also many sounds in the ocean that are *above* the range of human hearing.

Scientists know that some fish make sounds. There must be a reason why the fish make these sounds. Do you know the reason? Think about the bats and you may find a clue.

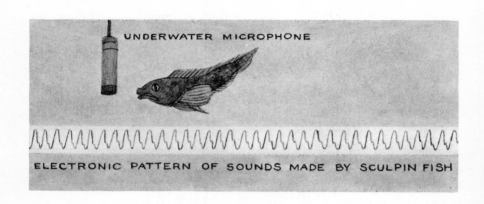

UNDERWATER MICROPHONE

ELECTRONIC PATTERN OF SOUNDS MADE BY SCULPIN FISH

Scientists believe that some of the deep-sea fish which travel in the darkest depths of the ocean, find their way around by listening to echoes of their own voices. That's what bats do, isn't it?

Fish are able to hear quite well, but they do not have ears like ours. They hear in a very unusual way. Sound waves pass through the *bodies* of fish to their *inner ears*. They have no ears on the *outside* of their heads at all.

Scientists also tell us that some whales "talk" to each other even though they do not have vocal cords that vibrate and produce sound, like ours. Sometimes they make very loud, strong sounds. Then they make clicking sounds—click, click, click—over and over again. The echoes of their clicks help to guide them through the sea.

The whale has some relatives that look as if they might be his small cousins. They are the porpoises, or dolphins, and they are great "talkers," too.

Porpoises squeak, grunt, and squeal. Some of the sounds porpoises make are high-frequency sounds that we could not hear without the use of electronic equipment. Porpoises are able to "hear" sounds which have a frequency of 150,000 vibrations a second. This is certainly in the ultrasonic range.

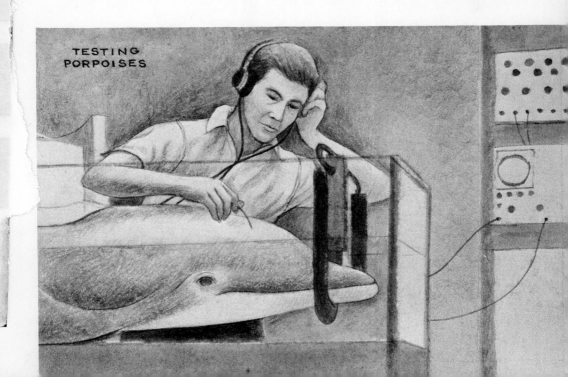

TESTING
PORPOISES

Both whales and porpoises make sounds when hunting for food in the dark, muddy water. Scientists are quite sure that they often "swim blind," using only the echo of their voices to guide them.

Even though we now know that there are talking creatures in the ocean, there is still a great deal to be learned about sounds in the *unsilent* world of the sea.

PORPOISES AND BLUE WHALES

8.

DO BIRDS FLY BLIND?

One foggy night at sea, several miles off the coast, a ship's captain received a report that something unexpected was happening on the radar scope. An unusual pattern was sweeping across the screen.

At first, the radar operator thought that it might be a group of airplanes flying in formation. But he soon realized that the strange pattern on the scope was caused

by a flock of wild geese that had flown within the detection range of the radar antenna.

The radar operator reported that the geese were flying at a speed of thirty-five miles an hour. That's fast—particularly on a night that was so foggy you could hardly see your hand in front of your face.

Were the geese flying blind? Scientists who study birds have wondered for a long time whether some birds

HERRING GULL

WILSON'S PETREL

depend on their hearing, rather than their sight, when they fly or hunt.

Think about the gannets. These sea birds dive from a height of one hundred feet, and then plunge into the sea for fish. Gannets have been captured in the nets of fishermen about ninety feet down in the sea. Surely, they could not see down there. Did they guide themselves by echoes? Scientists are not sure.

GANNET

NIGHTHAWK

LONG-EARED OWL

GUACHARO

Land birds also travel great distances under conditions where sight alone could not guide them. Young birds, hatched in the north, find their way south over thousands of miles of unknown country. Many of them "fly blind" over the ocean at night. Does their hearing help them find their way?

It is likely that the common nighthawk uses his ears to help him hunt. He lives on tiny insects that he catches in the dead of night—insects that he could not possibly *see*.

There is evidence that at least some birds really do depend upon sound—ultrasonic sound—to fly and hunt. There are cave-dwelling birds, the guacharos (gwa-CHA-roes), who live in South America. They sleep all day and, like the bats, they dart in and out of their dark caves without crash landings or accidents. And like the bats, they depend on the echoes of their ultrasonic clickings to navigate.

The long-eared barn owl also sleeps all day and awakens to hunt his prey at night. Suddenly, he dives down for the kill. A split second later he is clutching a tasty mouse in his beak.

How did the barn owl find his prey in the dark? He heard it, of course! Those long ears of his are not just there for decoration. The long-eared barn owl has

51

a keen sense of hearing. As a mouse runs over twigs and leaves on the ground, the barn owl *hears* the *faint* rustling sound—a sound that we would *never* hear.

Scientists are still not sure how much certain birds depend upon their sense of hearing, or whether many of them make use of ultrasonic sound. But they are finding out more each day.

9.

OCEAN

OBSTACLE COURSE

On an April night in 1912, a world-famous luxury liner descended to her watery grave. She was the *Titanic*.

It was a truly dark night. The stars were hidden behind a thick blanket of clouds. The face of the moon was masked in total darkness.

The ship was moving along at twenty-two knots. Several warnings of dangerous icebergs in the area had been received by the radio operator.

Suddenly, it happened! The *Titanic* struck a huge iceberg. Passengers became panic-stricken. The deep hum of the powerful motors ceased. Within three hours, the *Titanic* was resting on the ocean floor.

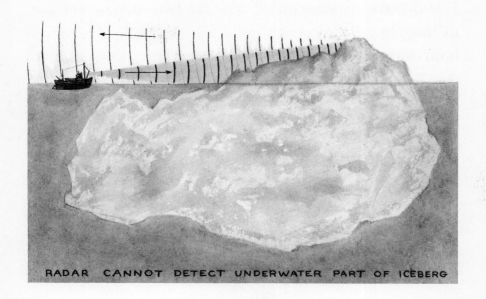

RADAR CANNOT DETECT UNDERWATER PART OF ICEBERG

Icebergs have long been of great danger to ships. The largest part of an iceberg lies below the surface of the water and cannot be seen. In foggy weather, even the top of an iceberg can hardly be seen if it is more than three hundred feet away.

For many years, icebergs were located by listening for echoes from a ship's horn. But such air-borne echoes couldn't detect the most dangerous part of an iceberg beneath the surface.

Do you think radar is useful in finding icebergs? It isn't, because radar does not work very well under water.

Radio waves cannot travel very far beneath the surface of the sea.

To locate an iceberg in time to save lives, man needed something that could travel below the surface of the water to detect underwater objects. Only with such a "tool" could he prevent disasters like the sinking of the *Titanic*.

Let's go back to the fifteenth century for a moment. Leonardo da Vinci, an Italian artist and scientist, put

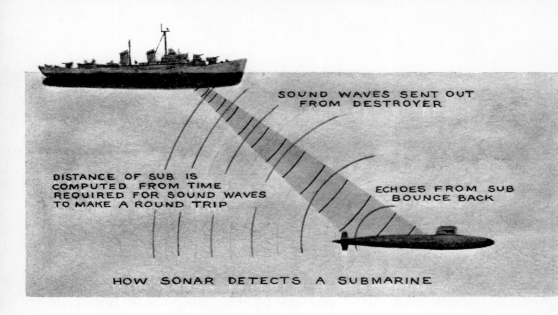

SOUND WAVES SENT OUT
FROM DESTROYER

DISTANCE OF SUB IS
COMPUTED FROM TIME
REQUIRED FOR SOUND WAVES
TO MAKE A ROUND TRIP

ECHOES FROM SUB
BOUNCE BACK

HOW SONAR DETECTS A SUBMARINE

one end of a long hollow tube into the sea. He held
the other end of the tube close to his ear. In this way,
Leonardo was able to hear ships which were great distances away. The sound vibrations made by the distant
ships moved through the water.

In the early twentieth century, scientists discovered
that *echoes* of *sound waves* could be used for the underwater detection of icebergs and other objects. This
discovery led to the invention of *sonar*. Sonar stands for
*SO*und *N*avigation *A*nd *R*anging.

Sonar makes use of high-frequency sound waves because these ultrasonic waves do not "get lost" among
the many low-frequency sound waves that are always
present.

Do you remember that regular sound travels in all directions? High-frequency sound is more useful in sonar because it can be aimed in one direction—just as a bullet or a beam of light can be aimed at something.

Sonar plays an important role in the defense of our country. It is our best tool for the detection of submarines. A destroyer, equipped with sonar, can search the depths for unwanted subs.

A device called a *transducer* changes electrical energy into high-frequency sound waves and sends them out into the ocean. Unheard by the sub, these high-frequency sound waves pulse—pulse—pulse through the sea. The speeding sound waves strike the sub's hull and bounce back toward the surface.

The transducer on the destroyer picks up the echoes. It changes these reflected sound waves back into electrical energy which is then sent to the sonar receiver.

The location of the sub can be computed by measuring the time it takes for the sound waves to reach the sub and bounce back.

Sound travels through the ocean at about 4,800 feet a second. If the round trip of the sound waves takes two seconds—one second each way—the target is about 4,800 feet away.

Since the invention of high-speed nuclear-propelled subs, sonar has become very important. It is often the only possible way of detecting such a submarine.

Modern submarines lurk far beneath the surface, where periscopes are useless. They cannot see, so they must hear. With sonar, a sub can hear without being heard.

Sonar is also now being used to help the blind. A sound projector (transducer) that sends out clicking sounds is attached to a blind person's belt or clothing. He listens for the echoes of the clicks. This helps him to keep from bumping into things.

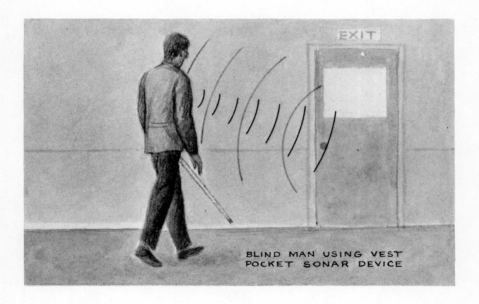

BLIND MAN USING VEST POCKET SONAR DEVICE

These projectors still need to be improved. They are not very useful in noisy areas. Outside noise makes it difficult for the blind person to hear the echoes.

The job of detecting obstacles is only one of the ways in which we can use high-frequency sound waves. Very soon, ultrasonics may become a vital part of our everyday lives.

10.

ULTRASONICS: TODAY AND TOMORROW

Medical researchers are experimenting with ultrasonics to help cancer victims. They are trying to find out if ultrasonics can detect cancer in human beings before it becomes too serious. Some scientists think that high-frequency sound waves might even be sent through the body to kill cancer.

It is already known that echoes are helpful in detecting tumors. Doctors are experimenting with ultrasonics to cure brain conditions in cases where an operation would not be helpful. Perhaps high-frequency sound waves can be used to kill brain tumors.

Ultrasonic energy has been known to lessen pain in illnesses like rheumatism and arthritis.

Ultrasonic rays, aimed at a surgical wound, speed up the healing process and help to avoid scars after an operation.

An ultrasonic drill has been invented for use in dentistry. A transducer makes the drill vibrate very rapidly. Instead of spinning, the drill vibrates up and down.

When a dentist uses an ultrasonic drill he applies it very lightly. Filling teeth the ultrasonic way is *fast* and *painless*. How about that?

Did you know that ultrasonic echoes are able to find flaws or faults in metals used for manufacturing? An electronic device called an *echo-ranger* sends out pulses of high-frequency sound and receives the returning echoes.

A beam of high-frequency sound is able to travel through more than forty feet of metal. When there is a flaw in the metal, a small echo bounces back after hitting it. The final echo returns from the very end of the metal.

Echo-ranging is also used to find faults in factory machinery. The machines do not have to be taken apart to find the source of trouble. As you can see, this saves time and money.

Ultrasonic waves are used in detecting flaws because low-frequency sound waves will bend around a small

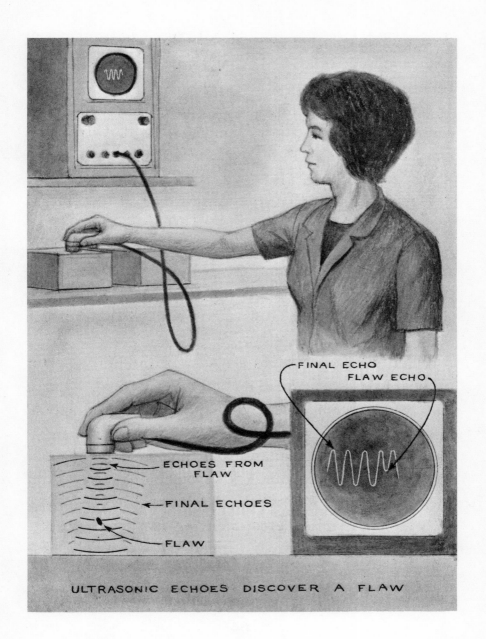

FINAL ECHO
FLAW ECHO

ECHOES FROM
FLAW

FINAL ECHOES

FLAW

ULTRASONIC ECHOES DISCOVER A FLAW

flaw and keep on going ahead. But ultrasonics will bounce off even tiny flaws that would be almost impossible to detect in any other way.

Another good thing about using high-frequency sound waves is that they cannot be heard. Ultrasonics can be used in factories without causing unbearable noise.

Did you know that the dishwasher of the future will clean without soap or suds? Dishes will be washed in a clear liquid by *bubbles.* Jewelry and surgical instruments will be cleaned in this way, too. You might think that the instruments are being boiled. But the liquid is *not* boiling. It is made active by ultrasonic waves.

When ultrasonic waves are forced through water or other liquids, very small bubbles are formed. After a split second, the bubbles collapse. Because of this action, great pressure is created in the liquid.

Bubbles form and collapse, over and over again, about 100,000 times a second. A kind of boiling occurs—but there is no heat. It is what we might call *cold boiling.* This gives the liquid great *cleaning power.* These tiny bubbles can reach into very small cracks and holes that cannot be cleaned any other way.

The ability of high-frequency sound to make bubbles is called *cavitation* because these tiny bubbles are actually spaces or cavities. Ultrasonic cavitation occurs so fast, and the bubbles are so small that you cannot see the movement of the liquid at all.

Ultrasonic waves are also being used to make our meat more tender. Frozen meat is put into salt water. High-frequency sound is sent through the water. The water's bubbling action helps to loosen the tough fibers of the meat. Cavitation makes the meat more tender without spoiling the flavor.

New uses for ultrasonics are being found each day— uses that will help us live healthier, pleasanter lives.

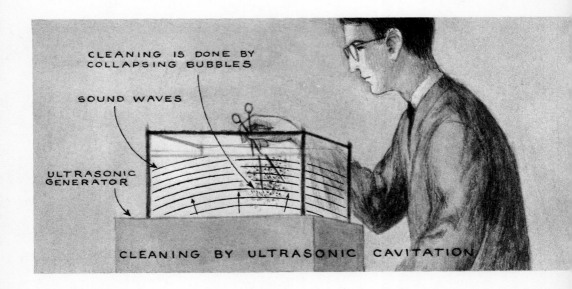

CLEANING IS DONE BY COLLAPSING BUBBLES

SOUND WAVES

ULTRASONIC GENERATOR

CLEANING BY ULTRASONIC CAVITATION

INDEX

67

68

P-H
JUNIOR
RESEARCH
BOOKS